SNOWFLAKES

• FOR ALL SEASONS •

64 fold and cut paper snowflakes

By Cindy Higham

This is a new and expanded edition.

Previous title was *Snowflakes made easy and fun.*

Salt Lake City, Utah

Library of Congress Catalog Card number: 98-92900

ISBN: 0-9664524-0-2

Copyright ©1998 By Cindy Higham

Graphic Design by ESB

INDEX

I've often heard that no two snowflakes are alike. That's also true with paper snowflakes. The slightest change in the paper folding or the slightest cut difference and you can have a new and exciting snowflake.

Use the patterns in the book to learn the techniques, then start experimenting on your own.

This could be the least expensive decoration you can make. Any 8½" x 11" sheet of paper will due and keep in mind that the paper doesn't have to be white. There are many paper styles and colors available to choose from. Find some paper and a pair of _sharp_ scissors and you're ready to start.

Use the diagrams at the bottom of this page to learn how to fold your paper. Then pick the pattern you want to try first.

You can use the same patterns many times. Xerox or trace the patterns rather than cut them out, and you'll have them to use over and over again.

You can also xerox your patterns smaller or larger so you have a variety of sizes of snowflakes to decorate with. Cut a piece of paper to the size you want your snowflake. Fold the paper, as per the instructions, then enlarge or reduce the pattern to fit your snowflake triangle.

HINTS

Put a small piece of tape on the sides of your folded paper this will hold it in place. Cut the small sections out 1st and work your way up to the large cuts–this will give you more paper to hold on to for a longer amount of time. You can tape the finished snowflakes to your windows or hang them from the ceiling with thread. Watch the room transform into a magical place.

If your snowflakes aren't flat you can press them into a book for a few days or you can take a "slightly warm" iron and press the folds out.

FAMILY FUN

If you want to make your SNOWFLAKES SPARKLE, you can buy glue sticks with glitter in them or glue glitter pens that are fun to decorate with.

It's fun to use colored paper based on the holiday you are cutting a snowflake out for. Such as green for St. Patricks Day or black or orange for Halloween.

Be creative, you'll think of several ways to decorate and display the snowflakes you create.

ADDITIONAL PRODUCTS

There are rubber stamps of many of our winter snowflakes now available by contacting:

Fantasy Impressions
4233 Howell Street
Philadelphia, Pa, 19135
(215) 744-3159

We will soon have computer clip-art available. Let us know if you are interested in purchasing a set.

For additional information on the clip-art, additional copies of book #1 or #2, or information about any of our products please call (801) 263-2336 or Fax (801) 263-2533

GOOD LUCK AND HAVE FUN!

PAPER FOLDING INSTRUCTIONS

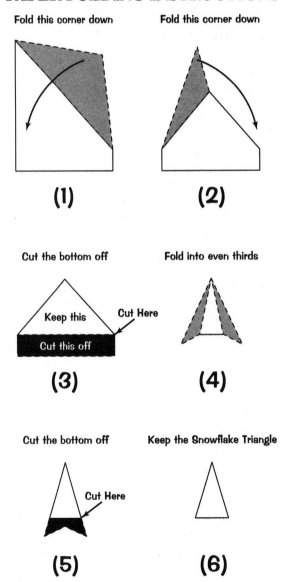

Fold this corner down   Fold this corner down

(1)   **(2)**

Cut the bottom off   Fold into even thirds

Keep this   Cut Here

Cut this off

(3)   **(4)**

Cut the bottom off   Keep the Snowflake Triangle

Cut Here

(5)   **(6)**

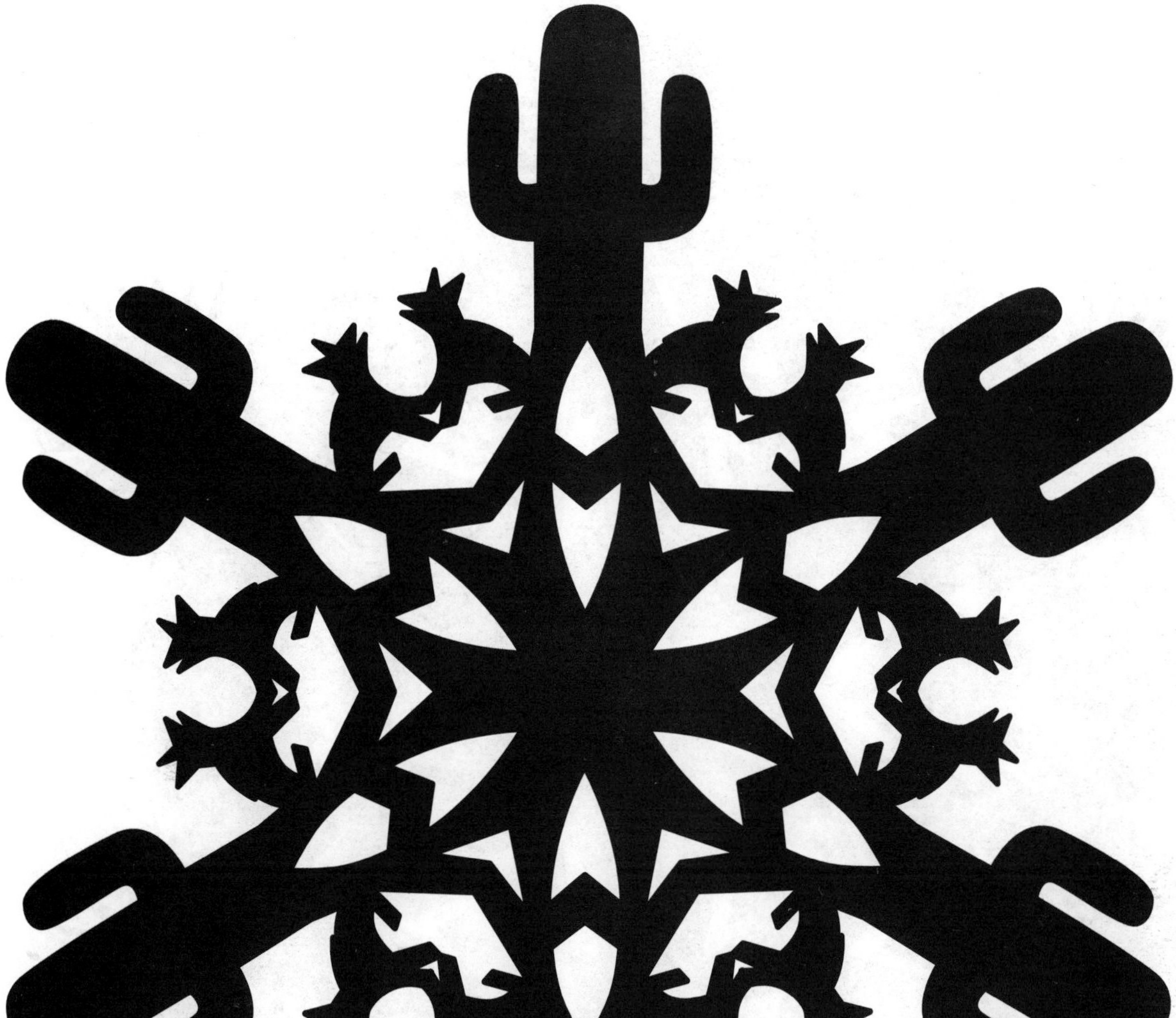

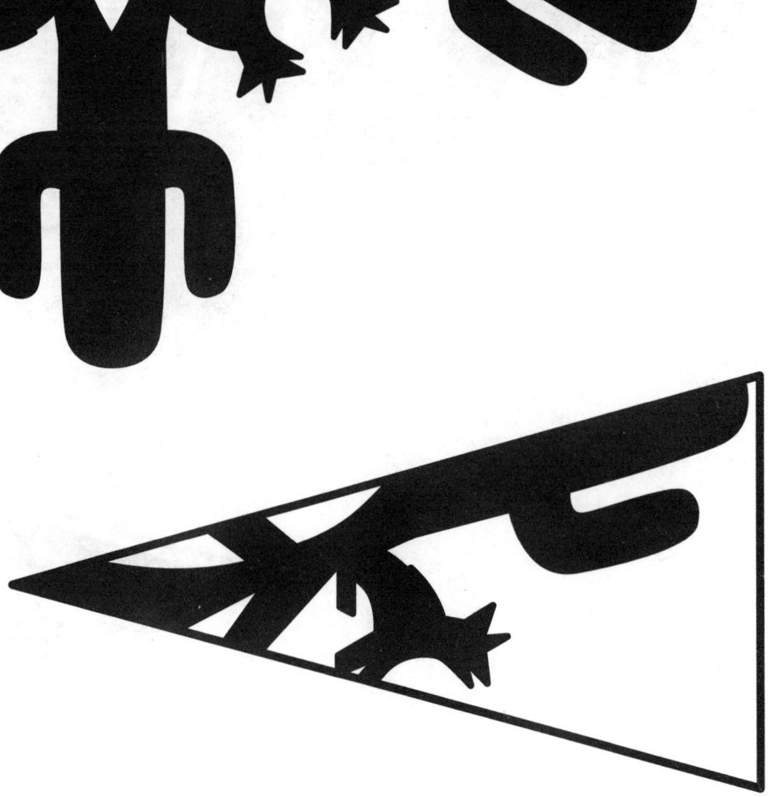

29

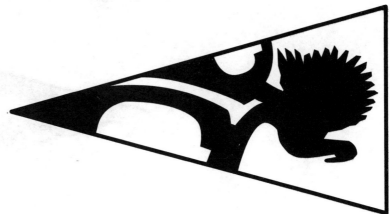

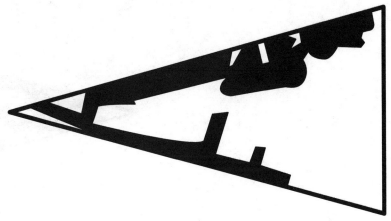

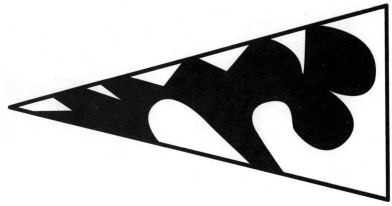